BEHIND THE LENDER'S DESK

A Reference Guide For Commercial Bank Lenders And Business Borrowers

BEHIND THE LENDER'S DESK

A Reference Guide
For Commercial
Bank Lenders
And
Business Borrowers

R. RANDY VEILLON

Parker House Publishing

Dedication

This book is dedicated to my mother,
Maude Rozas Veillon,
and to my brother,
V. Bradley Veillon.

Foreword

"The secret for harvesting from existence the greatest fruitfulness and the greatest enjoyment is — to live dangerously!"
~ Walter Kaufmann, *The Accidental City*, Lawrence N. Powell

Writing this book became a necessity for me, not so much to make money from sales, gain a reputation as a topic authority, or from the idea of getting my name in print (though all of those things sound fine, to be sure). I mainly wanted to provide guidance to those types of lenders and borrowers that I know will need it most, and for the sake of helping the scrappy and innovative young companies with sound potential to understand the process, know how to recognize and articulate their own innate potential and find the right loan opportunity to take their businesses (on either side of the table) to the next level.

Today's lending environment does *not* always have the clarity of vision to see the potential lurking in the shadows of a hastily scrawled business plan backed by invisible genius waiting in the wings. The most innovative or sound business does *not* always get the loan, due to how they appear on paper. There are legitimate reasons for this, however, as we shall see later in this book.

My aim, then, in relation to the loan applicant, as well as the lender, is to guide him or her through the proverbial dark woods, up to the safe entry point by which to enter the labyrinth of sound loans. There are perils awaiting the unwary, and hopefully you will reach for this book as a trusted guide through such winding and dark wooded paths. I urge you not to succumb blindly to fear. The paths generally do converge ahead as clarity and insight into the lending process and rationale are attained. And so those many, divergent paths all lead, not only to premature surrender in the face of confusion, but to a single converging road, into a clearing, and thus to all the potential ingredients for your best success.

The creative nerve is perhaps no more important (or tested) than in the founding of a business, or in its rise toward the well-capitalized heights of productivity after a long healthy proving period. This book can act as the humble honing stone against which your lending instincts can be sharpened, so that you can learn the difference between a company owner grown cocky from too narrow a range of business experience and the kind of seasoned company that is a spring awaiting to leap into its full productive powers. The loan cases contained herein reflect long experience in the lending industry from behind the lender's side of the desk. The scattered chestnuts that adorn these in various corners of this book are there to help bring out the full value of these cases as meditations on the essential, yet hard-to-define, nature of the bankable loan case.

I recommend a delicious cup of hot coffee when reading this book while seated in a comfortable chair, in a quiet room (I can imagine a gently crackling fireplace or a sleeping pet nearby), and with a lack of distractions as you plot the course of your Odyssey into what should properly be—by all rights—a thoroughly sober but thoroughly enjoyable business *adventure*.

Contents

Introduction

Business banking is about building solid relationships. Lenders want to help clients with viable businesses to succeed. Whether a client is buying a piece of equipment, real estate, or simply needs capital to grow, bankers want to help their customers finance their dreams. Their main requirement is that the loan makes sense on paper.

This book is not a technical credit analysis review. It is a basic, no-nonsense look at the way that I have reviewed loan requests for my own valued clients using the all-important Five C's of Credit: Capacity, Capital, Collateral, Character and Conditions.

This book is intended as a primer for any new commercial lender or branch manager and as a brush-up review for the more experienced lender. The case studies cited have been written in a simplified format for ease of understanding the loan requests presented.

What are loan officers looking for when approached about a loan? Here are some basic assumptions that an individual or business might be expected to provide a lender.

The business owner should have enough assets to handle bumps in business trends along with a sufficient reserve of cash.

An existing business owner must prove at least three years of positive cash flow to repay the loan request.

A start-up business will need an SBA Guaranty or other credit worthy guarantor to get the loan approved. Any new business, in fact, needs to show it has a track record of profitability and success in its business sector.

Initially, a commercial loan officer needs to know *which* financial statements are important.

Some basic terms:

- <u>Balance Sheet</u> - This statement shows the financial conditions of the business at a point in time.

- <u>Statement of Operations (Profit and Loss Statement)</u> - This statement shows whether the business has made a profit during a specific period of time.

- <u>Cash Flow Statement</u> - This statement shows what happened to the cash position during a specific period of time.

- <u>Cash Flow Projection</u> – This is a crucial financial management tool that must be developed with very realistic expectations. Sufficient cash is critical for a business to pay its expenses and to enable it to expand.

- <u>RLOC</u> – An acronym for "Revolving Line of Credit" (such as a personal or business credit card).

R. Randy Veillon

What to expect from this book

While this book does not aspire to the literary heights, it does aim to arm the average lender or loan applicant with the benefit of the lessons and insights of many years of brass tacks experience, provided in a simple and straightforward style. I hope the reader can not only appreciate the experience of reading this little book, but will take full advantage of the tips and insights gleaned from my own hard-won experience in the lending industry. Comments are welcomed in the form of your honest reviews.

"*The man who does not read has no advantage over the man who cannot read.*"
~ Mark Twain

A Brief and Entirely Arbitrary History of US Lending

If money is indeed the root of all evil, perhaps it is at least in part because to *not* have it (in a society that demands money as the accepted form of exchange) is not exactly a good omen for starting a business. Growth-friendly businesses are capital-thirsty, no matter how many good things they may do for a local community or for the world at large. Borrowing is a necessary step for all businesses launched by aspiring new entrepreneurs who don't have wealth of their own to use or who, by some outlandish streak of caution, prefer not to.

Since the dawn of the first depository notes used in the Bronze Age, humankind has had some relationship to money and thus to borrowing and lending money. With the founding of the colonies, all the way through abolition, banking, whether via state banks or the evolving national bank (The Federal Reserve Bank), and throughout the fluctuating hodge-podge of disparate currencies that led up to the current US dollar, and lending and borrowing have always been essential to both companies and economies, from the national level down to the small rural community.

In 1929, market instabilities erupted, followed by the Great Depression of the '30s. Family heads of households lacked jobs, because companies folded left and right. Banks had runs that morphed into house foreclosures. Not some but most suffered from the devastation. The federal government instituted banking reforms, along with public spending and safety net programs, and the economy limped along into World War II where, ironically enough, business opportunities and financial leverage lurked just around D-Day, on the beaches of Normandy in June of 1944. The air of optimism that erupted from the successful end of the war created an unstoppable market boom and capital flowed once again into the 1970's, until mishaps and squabbles over geopolitics and resources threatened to hamper the general national economic outlook. In the 80's, pro-business moves led to another market rally, which emboldened lenders throughout the 00's and right into the mirages of subprime lending and the monumental popping of the over-inflated housing super-bubble.

Today, at this writing (December 2015), the economy has for all intents and purposes appeared to have recovered some of its vigor, but with a newly heightened sense of caution. Along the way to this stage in lending history, many lessons have been registered and a price has been paid by the lender and borrower, alike. The banking environment of the

United States today is highly regulated by the FDIC and OCC, making it more difficult for a small business to get started without guaranty assistance from the SBA or USDA or a wealthy guarantor.

We are back to lending basics, with guidelines like cash flow positive at 1:25 to 1, and then there is the "75 to 80% loan to value" (LTV) rule on collateral. There is also the matter of the consideration of whether the loan request appeals to basic common sense (is it a crazy idea in unchartered territory...or a brilliant expansion upon proven principles in a hot new niche that is perfectly ripened for a windfall?). Lending has become more scrutinizing, and risks are ultimately not rewarded as readily. Angel investors and crowd-funding are new routes that have emerged in this climate. But both are often insufficient and take too long, as well as subjecting the business to what may be termed the "sexiness" test of the business idea, which in itself can be the least relevant thing to profitability or a sound business model.

The number of deals that banks go after today is getting smaller every year due to what many in the lending industry would call *over*-regulation. Regulations decrease the number of businesses they may legally lend to according to criteria that are increasingly defined and expanded upon by the federal government, to prevent such catastrophes as the 2007-2008 US recession.

After this most recent recession, the banking industry has seemingly come full circle. We are back to a situation where the perceived threats of lending are at something near the highest ebb (as the threat of a market crash is an unthinkable outcome) and the likelihood of getting a loan is at the lowest ebb perhaps in decades.

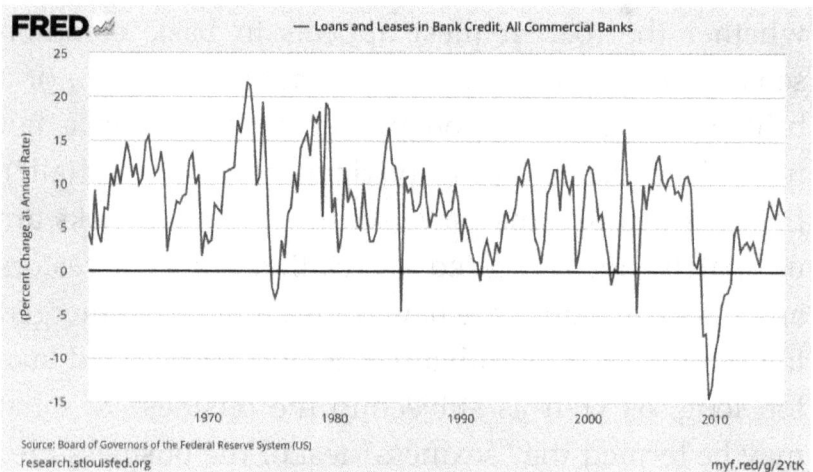

Percent and changes at annual rate

Now let's look at the chart displaying the rise and fall of commercial lending by the end of 2009, well after the recent 2007-2008 recession had done its damage.

See that sharp drop? It has recovered a little since then, but that initial peak before the drop marks the cycle high point since before 1974, letting you know

10

that things were both at an all-time-high and at an all-time-risk.

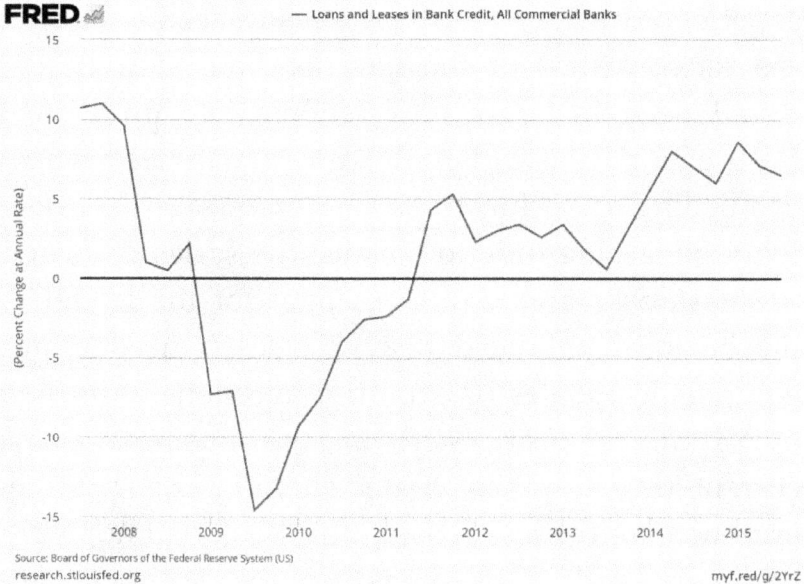

Loans and leases in bank credit, all commercial banks

Banks now typically demand that the business have three years of *consistent* positive cash flows to get a business loan deal approved, which does take into account measures of stability, but not of the fleeting nature of emerging opportunity. Banks are motivated to give priority towards the larger deals (with biggest profits), which they like better in terms of security factors and easy likelihood of success. The trend is more non-banks giving the loans that banks used to issue. That is the reality because of the stringent standards now in place.

This train of events is exactly why the new or less experienced lender or borrower may need a guide in the rocky waters of the new lending environment. You'll need to know how lenders now measure a fresh new business plan. Borrowers will need a truly compelling case for their loan request. That may require learning how to balance the scales of current business risks and profit potential for the lender. Is the business overhead heavy? Does it need critical equipment updates or expertise injections? Are there opportunities overlooked in the business plan's current trajectory that really should be part of the argument *for* the loan? Using this book will hopefully jar many such realizations for the borrower and lender alike. In the end, this book is about *helping good business loans to happen,* for the sake of both.

As the second chart shows, however, there is probably more hope ahead. And thus more reasons to try to squeeze that well-deserved loan in. You'll need to make sure it meets all the criteria laid out ahead. First, we'll start with marketing.

Marketing

Overcoming buying habits is difficult. However, once you realize that the majority of people locate any new product or service based on personal recommendations, not advertising, you have at least half the battle won. To win the other half, you must make your loyal customers, employees, suppliers and friends an integral part of your marketing plan so that your business will be recommended enthusiastically and often.

[Marketing Without Advertising, Michael Phillips and Salli Rasberry, Chapter 2, p. 5]

Advertising

Advertising can remind customers and prospects about the benefits of your product or service. You have to identify what is unique about your business and how that uniqueness will benefit the customer. This theme or image for your product or service will carry though all of your advertising and promotion. It is what sets you apart from the competition and it is what will attract the customer. Consumers are attracted by benefits.

Advertising allows you to have complete control. Unlike publicity, you have the final word in determining where, when and how often your message will appear, how it will look and what it will say.

[Target Marketing, Linda Pinson and Jerry Jinett, Third Edition, Chapter 10, page 26]

What Management Is

How should companies organize? Where should the lines be drawn? Bigger or smaller? The design of an organization is implicit in its strategy, so much so that it is sometimes hard to tell where strategy leaves off and organization begins. Because strategy is dynamic, organizations must be flexible. Drawing the lines of organization is an ongoing struggle to stay relevant, not a job done once and for all.

More than anything else, where the lines are drawn depends on what the organization is trying to accomplish, on how it is trying to do better by being different. A clear strategy thus becomes a kind of blueprint for an organization's design, shaping the most basic decisions about its scope, its scale, and its structure.

[What Management Is, Joan Magretta, Chapter 4, p. 96]

Marketing to the Customer

A **customer orientation** is where staff has a real concern for the customer and where all business decisions are made with a view to improving customer service. To orientate business activities successfully towards its customers, both staff and managers must:

- Listen closely to customer feedback.
- Understand and use customer needs, wishes and expectations as a basis for their activities.
- Understand the logic of the customer's business.
- Have insight into the customer's assessment criteria and act on them.
- Know and understand how and why the customer gives priority to a certain supplier.

Customer orientating a business means wearing customer spectacles and seeing with the customer's eyes. It's a matter of listening actively both to what the customer says and to what he or she does not say.

[Quality of Service, Bo Edvardson, Chapter 5, pp. 118-119]

Networking: A World of Unlimited Resources

A network is built on a foundation of mutual trust and support among members. Participants come together because of common interests and objectives, and they voluntarily give of themselves, because they know that by helping others they will eventually end up helping themselves.

[Marketing to Win, Frank K. Sonnenberg Chapter 6, pp. 75-77]

Boldly Marketing the Brand

Visibility pays because visibility has a halo effect. If a company or product is visible and well-known, we tend to think it is better than one that is not well known...think about it. When we buy something in a new category, we're likely to choose a brand we are familiar with.

[Breakthrough Branding, Catherine Kaputa, Chapter 7, p. 135]

Survival of the Fittest

Open your eyes – the world around you is changing at an unprecedented rate. The globalization of products and services and the deregulation of markets are altering the very nature of competition. You either recognize these dramatic changes and adapt or forget about competing successfully in the new marketing era.

[Marketing to Win, Frank K. Sonnenberg, Chapter 1, pp. 1-2]

*"Most of the energy of political work is devoted
to correcting the effects of mismanagement
of government."*
~ Milton Friedman

Introduction to Loan Cases

Assumptions - Financial statements and taxes match, individual credit scores are generally above 700, cash flow is sufficient to repay the loan request at 1.25 to 1 and collateral is at 75% LTV (Loan to Value.)

Lenders, please review each case, and see if you would recommend these loans to your loan committee based on the assumptions cited above. Also, remember the 5 C's of Credit: Capacity, Capital, Collateral, Character and Conditions.

Each loan case is based on a real case example. The loan amounts, names, and locations have been dutifully fictionalized for purposes of this book.

R. Randy Veillon

"Successful investing is anticipating the
anticipations of others."
~ John Maynard Keynes

Loan Summary: Doe Farce Offshore Boat

Doe Farce Offshore Boat is a Texas company established in 1976. Its strategy is to provide professional services, with top quality personnel and equipment, via a loan of $4MM to purchase a working boat. The loan will amortize at 10 years. By possessing an experienced management and repair team, their vessel will be maintained in great condition for uninterrupted service. This will provide excellent services for long-term business relationships. The vessel they have chosen has unique features that will be expected by their customers. Doe Farce Offshore Boat, LLC, will be owned and operated by John A. Doe. He has several years' experience in the oil and gas sector. His company has serviced offshore supply vessels for many years. The company is in charge of many types of repairs and refurbishments including supply boats, which are currently working in the oil industry.

Questions:

1. **What are the chances of approval?**
   The oil business *is* volatile, but not necessarily for deep-water rigs.

2. **What are risks associated with this request?**
   New boat purchase needs refurbishing, but the company has an experienced repair team.

3. **Is location crucial?**
   Most boat companies are located toward the southeast Texas coast.

Loan Summary: Recycling

Recycling companies recycle paper, glass, metal, and plastics. In order to succeed in this business, the company has to purchase the equipment from a machine producer for $800,000 and the loan will term at 5 years. The equipment is usually used as a curbside, single-stream sorting system. The business demands that the company hire and add new employees. The business is competitive and new equipment is needed to foster growth of the company and capture market share to stay competitive.

Joe Properties was formed in 1974 to be a real estate holding company in Florida. It operates a single stream recycling MRF (materials recovery facility) for the processing of curbside recyclables. Single-stream refers to material arriving at the facility that has not been separated by commodity (paper, plastic, glass, metal, etc.). Once processed, the materials are marketed to various industries. The company is now receiving recyclable material from several states. Additional tonnage is added through new contracts with commercial companies and municipalities.

Questions:

1. **What are the chances of approval?**
   Good, because this company has existing contracts with government agencies.

2. **What is your opinion of the company?**
   Because recycling is still a relatively new industry sector, the collateral is an issue. In addition, the company is purchasing non-standard equipment (this means no known reliability that could normally be associated with machinery brands like Caterpillar, etc.).

3. **Is the company ripe for a merger or acquisition?**
   Yes, due to economies of scale.

Loan Summary: Boat Manufacturing

Water Boats is a new company requesting a $1,500,000 loan to purchase equipment to manufacture boats in Texas in 1976. The owners will inject cash equity of 20% required. Collateral offered will be a first security interest in equipment valued not less than $1,500,000. The company is projected to earn $3,500,000 in sales the first year with a net income before taxes of $945,000.

Water Boats will be owned and operated by five individuals. They have many years' experience in the boat building business. The company will lease and operate a recently vacated boat manufacturing facility in Texas. The outlook for Water Boats is enhanced due to the fact that the technical staff maintained by another company resides within the Texas community and is prepared to work. The purpose of this request is to acquire the necessary equipment for Water Boats to become operational.

Water Boats will be a sister company to Joe Boats of Texas Two, and has been in existence since 1971. Joe Boats' primary emphasis has been in providing high quality patented boats for commercial and recreational use.

Questions:

1. **Is management strong enough to keep this business competitive?**
   Yes. Management has been around a while in this business.

2. **Collateral?**
   Bank will need a USDA loan approved, which guarantees an 80% loss protection for the bank.

3. **Will local bank entertain loan request without USDA Guaranty?**
   No.

"If past history was all there was to the game, the richest people would be librarians."
~ Warren Buffet

Loan Summary: Big Surge Services

Big Surge Services was formed by John Doe. In 1972 this Mississippi company provides sales, service and rentals of commercial air compressors within the South Texas market. John Doe manages the business. The principal, John Doe, will provide an *in solido* guaranty. The bank loan is in the amount of $2,700,000 to purchase *rental* units.

John Doe has been in the commercial air compressor industry for over 10 years. Starting as a mechanic, he worked his way up to Operations Manager for one of the area's leading compressor companies. Over the years, he has developed a respectable knowledge base of sales, rentals, maintenance of machines and local customer contacts. In 1986 John Doe felt, with this knowledge along with the relationships with the manufacturers, the time was right to start his own company.

Its customer base includes primary companies that provide inland and offshore fabrication to the oil and gas industry. While at his previous employer, Mr. Doe developed great working relationships with both customers and representatives of the oil and gas companies. He was able to leverage those relationships to start his company. From the start, he represented Minus Compressors. This was important since many of his past customers used Minus Compressors' products.

John Doe's products range from skid-mounted units to larger units. Although Mr. Doe initially focused on sales and services for compressors, he recently began offering customers the option of long-term rental units. Customers like this because they have the flexibility of a variable cost and not having to worry about the upkeep and maintenance of machines.

Questions:

1. **What are the chances of approval?**
   Prospective business owner has good experience in business and has equity.

2. **Is collateral bankable?**
   Yes, but it is located offshore.

3. **Will an SBA Guaranty be needed?**
   Yes – due to the nature of the collateral and the fact that is located many miles offshore.

Loan Summary: Good Mix

Good Mix is a 1978 start-up company requesting a $1,500,000 loan to finance land, equipment, and trucks in Florida. The owners injected $250,000 into the business, and will have a 20% equity position prior to loan closing. Collateral offered will be a first mortgage on land and a first security interest in equipment valued not less than $1,500,000. Term of the commitment is three years for the term loan. The company is projected to earn $3,150,000 in sales the first year with a gross profit before taxes of $570,000. The company will generate sufficient cash flow with $500,000 in gross profit to service the debt. Both principals will personally guaranty the loan.

Mr. Joe Doe left the oil business to start a sand stone company. Because of his sales experience, Good Mix has become the largest brick company in Florida. Mr. Joe Doe heard contractors complaining about concrete companies and their inability to meet deadlines and work with their clients. He decided to leverage his contacts within his former industry to start a new concrete company. In addition to his local contacts with contractors and concrete finishers, he was able to utilize his exiting aggregate supplier to provide product to his new company.

Mr. Joe Doe has been able to secure commitments from several of his existing clients and additional commitments from prospective clients. To date, commitments from several builders have been obtained. In addition to these homebuilders, several smaller commercial projects have been unofficially "promised" to the new group.

Reliability of delivery along with product stability is key to success in the concrete business. The plant will be automated to make sure mix ratios are accurate. An experienced operator has been hired to oversee and ensure proper mixture levels.

Questions:

1. **Is location important?**
   Yes.

2. **Collateral?**
   The prospective business owner owns valuable real estate and equipment.

3. **Competition?**
   Yes, intense.

4. **Timing?**
   Real estate is moving very well in the year indicated.

Loan Summary: Car Crash Center

Car Crash Center is a new company—less than a year old—formed in April 1988 in the state of South Carolina. It has requested a $1,000,000 loan to finance the acquisition of the automobile body shop which it is currently leasing. The Collision Center is to be secured by land, building, equipment, and improvements. The owners will inject $250,000 cash into the business which meets the acquisition equity requirement for a 20% equity position. Collateral offered on Car Crash Center will be a first mortgage on land, building, equipment, and improvements which should value at $1,040,000 which is 80% loan to value on a loan of $1,300,000. Term of the commitment is set at five years for the term loan. The company is projected to earn $3,000,000 in sales the first year with a net profit after taxes of $600,000.

The business is a body shop. The company repairs automobiles and trucks and performs bodywork repairs. The business has three components: body shop for painting, sheet metal, and frame work. Also performed are alignments, tire repair and transmission services. Mr. Doe is the general manager of the company and Mr. Big Doe is his right hand man. Tom Trombone is in charge of customer service, customer contact, sales and handling documentation with insurance companies.

Questions:

1. **What are the chances of approval?**
   Good.

2. **Is management strong enough to make a successful business?**
   Yes, they have industry experience.

3. **Collateral?**
   General use valuable real estate.

Loan Summary: Seafood Sales

A seafood wholesaler seller distributes high quality wild-caught domestic seafood on a daily basis. The owner is requesting $7MM for a building with freezers and $1MM in working capital located in Florida in 1977. The company plans to offer high quality products and exemplary service to the food service industry. The owner knows the seafood industry well and will use past experience to build a successful business. He should be well aware of the U. S. Department of Commerce standards for Quality Assurance, implement and follow a rigorous sanitation standard, and adhere to the FDA's Hazard Analysis and Critical Control Point (HACCP) program for seafood safety.

The plant should be complete with cold storage and have the capacity to store a large inventory of seafood. It is common for a distributor to take in third party products to be blast frozen/stored.

The distributor usually buys shrimp off the docks direct from the boats and package for retail/wholesale sales. This is a business of pure supply and demand. If the distributor has a quality supply of fresh seafood, he can demand good prices. If management has an extensive knowledge in the marketing of seafood, the business bodes well for its success.

Questions:

1. **What are the chances of approval?**
   Good.

2. **Does he have the proper food regulatory bodies overseeing the business?**
   Yes. He has both state and federal oversight.

3. **Collateral?**
   Valuable real estate and equipment.

Loan Summary: Frozen Air

Frozen Air is a specialty air conditioning and refrigeration company offering both sales and rental of industrial and commercial HVAC equipment to local, national and global customers. The company was incorporated in 1974 in Houston. Owner is a seasoned manager and refrigeration tech by trade with over 25 years of experience in his trade.

The owner is requesting a $600,000 equipment loan and a $100,000 working capital loan for the first six months of operation. Mr. Todd has a loyal customer base and is well known in this industry. This industry is not just about renting items as much as it is an industry of providing solutions for temporary problems through the use of experience and technology, while providing high quality service. His company competes with about 15 companies within a 75-mile radius of Houston to service the 160 industrial plants on the river. The chiller and generator industry in Texas is approximately a $75,000,000 market annually. The company will be working with plant engineers, recovery departments and maintenance departments to assist them with their needs.

Questions:

1. **What are the chances of approval?**
   Good.

2. **Is good customer service important in this business?**
   Yes, but isn't that true for all businesses?

3. **Collateral?**
   Equipment.

Loan Summary: Educational Center

Educational Center was incorporated under the laws of Tennessee in 1989. It offers educational services to home schooled students and to traditionally schooled students.

This $200,000 loan request will go to fund inventory. Educational Center provides academic programs to home-schooled students from 3rd grade to 12th grade, tutoring programs for all students from kindergarten to graduate school, and test preparation for most standardized tests.

The company is owned by a teacher and employs four full-time and three part-time teachers. These teachers provide educational services to approximately 80 home-schooled students and to 50 tutoring students. Home-schooled classes meet two hours per day, Monday through Thursday.

Tutoring sessions are typically one hour in duration and are attended once or twice a week. Those sessions are offered Monday through Thursday from 3:30 p.m. to 7:30 p.m.

For the past two years, the company has operated at capacity and had to turn down 30 home-schooled students each year and at least as many tutoring students.

Questions:

1. **Is the school certified by the State of Tennessee?**
   Yes.

2. **How many students can the school accommodate?**
   120.

3. **Collateral?**
   Real estate.

Loan Summary: Fancy Properties

Fancy Properties was incorporated under the laws of Oklahoma in January 1979; it is in the business of land development. The company's income and expenses all relate to the ownership of rental property.

Fancy Properties is owned by an investor, a land broker with over 20 years' experience. He has owned and developed several tracts of land for over 30 years He needs to refinance his companies of about $15MM. The bank would term this deal at 10 years. His companies are used to purchase land, develop land, purchase and hold land for appreciation in price and resale. Operating procedures are normal research and feasibility studies for the land development. Balance sheets are prepared by an accountant once all estimates of development companies and cost are received. The accountant then calculates the breakdown and profits expected to be earned.

Management team includes his best friend who has been a real estate salesman for over 15 years and has been involved in all developments, sales and listings and has knowledge of all transactions of the company.

Owner is a proven operator with extensive experience in the land development business.

Questions:

1. **What are the chances of approval?**
   Depends on market and return on real estate investment.

2. **Is this a risky business?**
   General contractors are very risky.

3. **Collateral?**
   A/R progress payments.

4. **Timing?**
   Is this the best time to invest in real estate?

Loan Summary: Big Tech

Big Tech is an expanding business located in Texas. The company was established in 1989 as a regional marine diesel engine service company. Prior to this, the company name was Joe Big, which was established in 1972. Currently, Big Tech is a multi-faceted heavy-industrial and marine service company that provides sales, service, parts, and warranties for diesel engines. Owners are involved in the daily operations of the company.

The company has outgrown its old facility located in Houston, Texas. It is currently leasing a larger facility which is located on the other side of town. The company is currently turning new customers away due to an insufficient amount of facility space. The company is therefore requesting a $2MM loan for a new building to properly house all its equipment.

Questions:

1. **What are the chances of approval?**
   Good.

2. **Is company too narrowly focused?**

No, it does business with oil, gas and industrial sectors.

3. **What is the collateral?**
Valuable real estate.

"Good people do not need laws to tell them to act responsibly, while bad people will find a way around the laws."
~ Plato

Loan Summary: Large Foods

Large Foods is located in Texas. The loan is a real estate loan for $4,000,000, secured by real estate. The real estate loan will be cross pledged along with all leases and rents. The principals will provide *in solido* continuing guarantees.

Large Foods was formed in 1976 in Texas with the combination of two other existing businesses. Both of the other businesses were family-owned and each of the two principals purchased his respective business from his father to create the company.

The company operates a food service distributor servicing the companies in Texas. The full protein line consists of beef, lamb, veal, and pork. The seafood line consists of shrimp, fish, oysters, crawfish, lobsters, and crab meat. The company provides the products in bulk or they are made to order of the clients. Large Foods employs skilled butchers to custom-cut orders, which can save the client costs on portioned controlled meats costs. The company provides same-day delivery service within Texas. It has over 1,000 food vendors with 20,000 products at its disposal to handle any custom order that may arise. The company's client base consists of restaurants and other food outlets.

Questions:

1. **What are the chances of approval?**
    Good.

2. **Collateral position strong?**
    Valuable real estate. Also seafood and produce.

3. **Guarantor needed?**
    SBA will be needed for support.

Loan Summary: Cream Cold

Cream Cold (CC) is owned by Mr. John Dough and Mike Dough in Oklahoma and was built in 1973. CC needs $600,000 of term debt to purchase new equipment. The borrowers will manage and operate the store daily with no salary until they feel confident with sales volume. If they meet their projections with the new store, the plan is to open an additional shop.

CC began operations in San Francisco, CA, in 1967. The franchisor has expanded to 225 stores in 34 states including several company-owned shops. CC has been growing its sales of quality ice cream, and the popularity of mixing sweet desserts has increased. Quality ice cream accounted for a significant share of the billions of dollars Americans spend on ice cream.

Questions:

1. **What are the chances of approval?**
   Good.

2. **Is this industry sector growing?**
   Ice cream has grown into a high-end boutique type of business.

3. **Is this plan based on a product that consumers demand?**
   Yes.

"The people who are crazy enough to think they can change the world are the ones who do."
~ Steve Jobs

Loan Summary: Fleet Car Repair

Fleet Car Repair is a Florida Limited Liability Corporation that performs routine maintenance and heavy repair mechanical work on commercial vehicles and passenger cars and trucks. It was formed in January 1979 in Georgia and began operating that same year.

The company's request is for a term loan to purchase commercial real estate and construct a metal building that will be used as an automotive repair shop. The term loan amount is $2,000,000.

The loan will be secured by a first mortgage on the commercial real estate and new construction by Fleet Car Repair. The subject property is approximately 9 acres that will be improved with a newly constructed 10,500 square-foot commercial metal building to be used as an automotive repair shop. The bank will also perfect an interest in shop equipment via Security Agreement and UCC-1 Financing Statement.

The new facility will have 12 additional stalls with one being exclusively dedicated to the issuance of state inspection stickers. The current facility presently has four stalls with none currently being dedicated to state inspection. A waiting room will be provided with the new construction, as currently there is no place for customers to wait for quick routine maintenance or repairs. This expansion project will give the business the ability to store vehicles overnight when needed for more complicated repairs. Parking would be far better than at the present location. Demand is presently greater than capacity.

Questions:

1. **What are the chances of approval?**
   Good.

2. **Is this sector growing?**
   Yes, collision repair is a service that customers always need and the number of drivers is always on the rise in the average city.

3. **Collateral?**
   Good real estate.

Loan Summary: Small Oil Service

Small Oil Service (SOS) owner, Charles Doe, began operations in 1957 in Texas. His son, James, has been employed by the company since 1965. The father is no longer connected with SOS. The company needs $3MM to refinance the debt and get working capital for the next six months. The collateral consists of land, a building and related equipment.

SOS repairs and installs industrial boilers and furnaces for large industrial customers in the chemical and wood products industries throughout the Texas Coast region.

Since 1981, company management noted that a handful of events during the FYE severely damaged the company's financial results. Most of the problems centered on its shop fabrication, which is not their primary business, nor is it profitable. As a result, management has taken corrective action by limiting fabrication jobs to its core business, and changed personnel in the estimating, review process, and supervision areas. Management has also lowered major overhead expenses, making it a leaner company.

Owners took a salary cut, and two construction department manager positions were eliminated in

Texas. The company is now profitable and is growing market share.

Questions:

1. **What are the chances of approval?**
   Chances were questionable at first, but improved dramatically as the company achieved greater cost-efficiency.

2. **Is the collateral offered sufficient to cover the risk?**
   Yes, collateral based at a 2:1 ratio is sufficient.

Loan Summary: Big Corp.

Big Corp. (BC) is a corporation headquartered in Jackson, MS. The company was founded by Steven Remington in 1962. BC has evolved from a small PC shop to an advanced IT firm that integrates computer systems and applications over a secure network.

BC is currently housed in the Technology Center of Jackson Tech. The complex is a $47 million, 170,000 square-foot building and is one of the most comprehensive and tightly integrated data visualization and supercomputing installations in the world.

In addition, it is connected to the state optical Network Initiative fiber network that connects major state universities to the fiber backbone infrastructure throughout the world. Having access to the network and assets of the Technology Center's facilities creates a strategic advantage very few other companies would ever have access to. The company is a reseller of computer networking, internet advanced technology and communication equipment combined with high-margin value-added services. This value can come from professional services such as integrating customizing, consulting, training and implementation services. The company continued to achieve great success in building upon its core business with a $2MM term loan on new equipment for 7 years.

Questions:

1. **What are the chances of approval?**
   None.

2. **Is collateral bankable?**
   No.

Loan Summary: Oil Dock

Oil Dock (OD) began operations in 1965 in Mississippi. It provides dock construction and refurbishment services. The company sub-bids portions of work that configures and designs fireguards used on docks and platforms that impact surfaces of boats. Fireguards are rubber pads that protect the areas where boats and docks impact together. Optimum placement of these fireguards utilizes the skill sets of an engineer.

The company needs $3 million to produce the rubber pads. Projections indicate they must repay this deal within 5 years. OD's business model calls for submitting a bid for the engineering design and the supply of the recommended fireguards. When awarded a bid, OD orders the fully constructed fireguards from its supplier and ships them to the job site. The general contractor performs the installation. The foreign supply source is part of OD's competitive edge as foreign rubber materials are significantly less costly than domestic rubber materials. Management does have competition; however, they often win bids because of their pricing edge gained from using foreign suppliers.

Questions:

1. **What are the chances of approval?**
   Good.

2. **What is this loan secured with?**
   Inventory and equipment.

3. **Is there industry demand for this service?**
   Yes, both nationally and internationally.

Loan Summary: Oil Well Drilling

Oil Well Drilling is a limited liability company, incorporated under the laws of Oklahoma in 1982. The company is in the business of providing well drilling services.

Oil Well Drilling as the borrower, proposes the financing of $10,000,000 to be used for purchase of a new drilling rig and a working capital loan.

Oil Well Drilling has been serving the Texas area for over 25 years. The company has grown into an oilfield service company with 90 plus employees. The Rig Division was also added to accommodate the client companies with a package offering. This rig has been employed to drill and re-enter shallow oil wells and drilled salt-water disposal wells in Oklahoma and Texas.

Questions:

1. **Would you do this loan request?**
   Yes.

2. **What are risks associated with this request?**
   Oil and gas prices.

3. **Is management going in the right direction?**
    Yes.

4. **Is this a volatile business?**
    Very.

Loan Summary: School Academy

School Academy is a limited liability company, incorporated under the laws of Texas in 1968. The company is in the business of providing educational services to students.

The purpose of the business is an educational facility that will provide services to the Texas residential, commercial, and industrial community located within a ten-mile radius of the proposed facility location. Owners have been public school teachers and administrators for several years.

Based on area statistical data, a market exists for the company's continuation in the location.

The company requires a loan of $600,000 to facilitate the transaction with monthly payments of principal and interest on the term loan based on a 20-year amortization.

Mission is to provide quality educational services to the ever expanding residential surrounding area. Academy focuses on providing individualized educational services for K-12 students with an emphasis on convenient hours, as well as quality educational and social skills development.

The owner has experience dealing with children of all ages in a school setting. Last year, he began with only 10 students. The school completed its first academic year with 40 students. Of those 40, 38 are returning along with 8 new students. The company continues to receive phone calls and emails weekly about enrolling new students. They presently sublease three classrooms. They have outgrown that space and would like their own building.

Owner's overall vision is to grow the school to as many students as possible while adding teachers necessary to maintain the proper student/teacher ratio. When the student body outgrows the initial facility, a second construction loan will be needed to expand the facilities on the existing property. The business will be in compliance regarding the rules and regulations of the Texas State Department of Education Home School.

Questions:

1. **What are the chances of approval?**
   Good.

2. **Is collateral bankable**?
   Yes, valuable real estate.

3. **Why do they need to refinance?**
   Need longer term; SBA deal.

4. **Out-of-state borrower. Does bank have authority to make the loan?**
   Depends on bank policy.

R. Randy Veillon

"In the nature of things, the amateur investor remains and probably will remain at a certain disadvantage in relation to the professional. Perhaps his best protection lies in knowledge of that fact itself."

~ John Brooks

Loan Summary: Bone Clinic

Bone Clinic (BC) was incorporated under the laws of Tennessee in 1978. The company is in the business of providing rehabilitation services for medical patients. Owner required a $5MM loan to refinance the land and building over a 10-year payback.

BC operated as an inpatient rehabilitation hospital from 1978 through 1985. Changes in the healthcare reimbursement structure during that time found the company difficult to operate with the appropriate return in investment being a small independent provider. Investment return will be greater if leased to a provider who has multiple facilities.

BC is owned by a Georgia resident, a health care executive with over 30 years' experience. He has owned and developed several healthcare facilities beginning in Georgia.

Changes in the healthcare landscape over the years made it apparent that a small single provider of inpatient hospital services, even for a specialty hospital, was forced to increase overhead to meet new regulations at a rate faster than rate increases were able to be implemented. The trend meant that these facilities either had to increase the number of inpatient beds, or offer services to spread the additional overhead costs. By leasing the rehab hospital to a provider of multiple facilities, the company could achieve a more consistent rate of return on equity and assets.

Questions:

1. **What are the chances of approval?**
   Good.

2. **Is collateral bankable?**
   Yes, real estate.

3. **Why do they need to refinance?**
   Need longer term to compete.

4. **Out-of-state borrower. Does bank have authority to make the loan?**
   Depends on bank policy.

Loan Summary: Physical Therapy

Physical Therapy is a limited liability corporation, incorporated under the laws of Georgia in 1975. Physical Therapy is in the business of providing physical therapy services.

The company's owner is a physical therapist with over 20 years of experience. She has cultivated many relationships with doctors and hospitals throughout the Atlanta metropolitan area to grow her physical therapy businesses.

The Medicare changes were not fully outlined initially, and this impacted PT's revenues. Medicare altered the usual means of patient billing. Once the owner realized this, they were able to resume normal fee billing for patients. In addition, Workers' Compensation codes were also changed without advance notice, which forced her to re-file many of her claims.

She hired new personnel recently to properly administer payments, along with a new physical therapist. This gives her more time to focus on growing her physical therapy service.

Questions:

1. **What are the chances of approval?**
   Good. PT's medical business is tightly controlled.

2. **Structure and collateral?**
   Real estate with good loan to value.

Loan Summary: Billiards

Billiards Development is a limited liability corporation, incorporated under the laws of North Carolina. The company is in the business of family entertainment since 1965. Owner requested $5.6MM loan for land and building based on a 15-year amortization.

Owner has a Bachelor's Degree in Social Work from Florida State University. She has 23 years of supervisory experience in home health care. For the last eight years, she has owned and operated an in-home assisted living business with annual sales of $3.5 million dollars. Prior to that, she managed and coordinated services for clients in group home settings for 22 years.

Persons with mental retardation and dementia need a lot of social stimulation and interaction. This stimulation increases their social skills and reduces many forms of deviant behavior. There have been so few locations in the area market that they are always full and cannot accommodate handicapped individuals who come as a group.

Questions:

1. **What are the chances of approval?**

Good. LTC centers have good cash positions.

2. **Structure and collateral?**
   Real estate with USDA Guaranty.

"Money has little value to its possessor unless it also has value to others."
~ Leland Stanford

Loan Summary: Experimental

Experimental formed in 1967. The company is focused on technical research.

Experimental owner is a research scientist located in Alabama. She needs a loan of $10,000,000 to purchase and remodel a medical building. In addition, she needs $600,000 in working capital. The 1977 appraisal indicates a total value of $16,000,000. The company's research team will occupy one floor, and the company will lease out the other five floors.

Experimental is a privately owned technical research facility that collects crucial and vital trial data for pharmaceutical and biotech companies for submission to the FDA in order to get approval for new drugs and devices. Company is planning to replicate this model in another medical facility in Atlanta. The building to be purchased and renovated will be a repositioning opportunity of a 150,000-square-foot specialty healthcare building. It will be strategically positioned in one of the busiest medical centers in the nation with more than a million outpatient visits annually.

As an on-campus asset built in 1962, this extraordinary investment opportunity allows the investor to purchase a significant medical asset well-below cost; current appraisal at $16,000,000. This new facility is highly finished to include 62 semi-private rooms with a capacity of 400 patient beds and 44 restrooms, a technical laboratory and an on-site pharmacy.

Questions:

1. **What are the chances of approval?**
   Good, the applicants are medical doctors with strong Personal Financial Statement (PFS.)

2. **Appraisal value sufficient?**
   Yes, real Estate value at 55% LTV.

Reasons for Loan Rejection

Lack of Complete Business Plan – Most commercial loan officers expect a complete business plan with an Executive Summary. This makes it easier for a lender to make a good decision.

Lack of Collateral – Most commercial loan officers expect applicants to have enough assets like home equity, land, inventory, or business equipment to repay the loan.

Lack of Experience – Most commercial loan officers expect business borrowers to have management expertise in the business they want to own.

Lack of Credit History – Most commercial loan officers expect business borrowers to have a good credit history.

Lack of Cash Injection – Most commercial loan officers want borrowers to have "skin" in the loan request.

R. Randy Veillon

"Don't let the noise of others' opinions drown out your own inner voice. And most important, have the courage to follow your heart and intuition."
~ Steve Jobs

Outline for a Business Plan

There is no single formula for developing a business plan, but some elements are consistent throughout all business plans. A plan should include an executive summary, a description of the business, a plan for how the company will market and manage the business, financial projections and the appropriate supporting documents.

I have summarized the essential elements in the following outline:

1. Cover Letter
   a. Dollar amount requested
   b. Terms and timing of loan request
   c. Type and price of collateral
   d. Summary

2. Summary
   a. Business description
      1) Name
      2) Location and plant description
      3) Product
      4) Market and competition
      5) Management goals

3. Business Goals

73

4. Summary of financial needs and application of funds

5. Earnings projections and potential return to investors

6. Market Analysis
   a. Description of total market
   b. Industry trends
   c. Target market
   d. Competition

7. Products or Services
   a. Description of product line
   b. Proprietary position: patents, copyrights and legal and technical considerations
   c. Comparison to competitors' products

8. Manufacturing Process (if applicable)
   a. Materials
   b. Sources of supply
   c. Production methods

9. Marketing Strategy
   a. Overall strategy
   b. Pricing policy
   c. Sales terms

    d. Method of selling, distributing and servicing products

10. Management Plan
    a. Form of business organization
    b. Board of Directors composition
    c. Officers: organization chart and responsibilities
    d. Résumés of key personnel
    e. Staffing plan/number of employees
    f. Facilities plan/planned capital improvements
    g. Operating plan/schedule of upcoming work for the next one to two years

11. Financial Data
    a. Financial history (five years to present)
    b. Three-year financial projections by month.

        1) Profit and loss statements
        2) Balance sheets
        3) Cash flow charts
        4) Capital expenditures estimates

    c. Explanations of projections supported by a written narrative
    d. Key business ratios

e. Explanation of use and effect of new funds
f. Potential return to investors compared to competitors and industry in general

The Small Business Development Centers (SBDC), usually located near a college, offer no-cost, confidential consulting assistance customized to your needs. SBDC business consultants will help you evaluate your business idea, prepare marketing strategies, determine financing needs, develop a loan proposal, conduct industry and market research, and create an actionable business plan.

SBDC consultants have extensive experience and training in diverse industries and expertise in the areas of marketing, finance and management. All of them are experts who can help you develop and implement strategies to get - and keep - your business up and running. SBDC's are a free service.

Build a Case for the Business Plan

This age-old business plan maxim stands repeating: in the case for the business plan, thoughtful plan writing is a *must*.

Business plans usually have two objectives. The first objective is that the plan should tell you if something can be done. The second objective is that it indicates just *how* that "something" might take place.

The plan should be a "live" plan, which could change weekly or even daily depending on the type of industry you are pursuing. Read faithfully.

Key sample pointers for a business plan:
(BPplans.com)

- Marketing Vision
- Business Goals
- Tactical Goals
- Strategic Goals
- Purpose
- Ideal Customer
- Market Description
- Core Strategy
- Core Branding Elements
- Logo Colors

77

- Product/Service Innovation
- Price Rationale
- Marketing Materials
- Web Plan
- Social Media
- Lead Generation
- Referrals
- Service Experience
- Sales Forecast
- Marketing Expense Budget

Be independent and creative as you may have more pointers to fulfill for your particular business plan. Consistency and a strong narrative in support of your plan is key to articulating a compelling case from the bare facts of your loan case.

Important to remember: The marketing component of your business plan is the burning bush in your loan proposal. *The business plan alone cannot guarantee you a loan.* What your business plan, if properly written, could do is to get you in front of a lender/investor. At that point, *you* have to sell the lender/investor on your plan. He or she must be able to envision how your marketing plan within your overall business plan will draw in substantial revenue with excess room for growth in that revenue.

Once you put your ideas to paper, you will be surprised how quickly your business plan becomes a reality. Remember to make updates to the plan regularly.

Seems like a lot of stuff to remember? Perhaps, but if you want to get your business off the ground, the business plan is where you begin.

Rome wasn't built in a day. Everything that has ever been built in the history of mankind started with an idea, whether inspired by accident or by example. Railroads, the sciences, the arts, and finance itself would never have taken off if not for the initial stirrings of wishful thinking, followed by scrutinizing and finally a bit of hard work and disciplined dedication.

If you already have a business, consider how good you feel about the business and why. Why do your customers like the business? How could it be "the perfect machine"? Answering such questions can quickly set you on the road to the eventual stage of putting that loan proposal on the desk, and put you in the driver's seat of a bigger company to hand down to future generations.

"*Money is not the most important thing in the world.
Love is. Fortunately, I love money.*"
~ Jackie Mason

Business Lender's Loan Application Checklist:

✓ **Personal Background and Financial Statement**

✓ **Past three years' Balance Sheets and Profit and Loss (P&L) Financial Statements**

✓ **Projected Financial Statements** – For Startup or Expanding Businesses - include three years' worth of detailed monthly projections with cash budget of income and finances and attach a written narrative explanation as to how you expect to achieve these projections.

✓ **Business Certificate/License**

✓ **Loan Application History** – Include records of any loans you may have applied for in the past.

✓ **Income Tax Returns** – Include signed personal and business federal income tax returns of your business' principals for previous three years.

✓ **Résumés** – Include personal résumés for each principal.

✓ **Business Overview and History** – Provide a brief history of the business and its challenges.

✓ **Business Lease** – Include a copy of your business lease, or note from your landlord, giving terms of proposed lease.

✓ **Proposed Bill of Sale including Terms of Sale**

✓ **Collateral** – Asking price with schedule of land, building, equipment and inventory.

✓ **Cash** – if start-up, injection amount into business by borrower. Banks may require existing businesses to inject cash depending on the loan request, but usually go on the equity section of the business reflecting paid-in-capital, or retained earnings. Borrower must have credit score acceptable to lender.

✓ **Formal Business Plan/Executive Summary**

* **Some lender's may require additional information.**

The FAQ's Section

What does Veillon Business Consulting (VBC) offer to clients?

We offer business owners affordable strategies for growth, re-structure and capitalization.

What kind of loans does VBC offer?

We connect businesses with long-term loans with payback lengths of up to 20 years for start-ups or expanding businesses though our extensive network of bankers, alternative lenders, government loan guarantees, and enormous commercial lenders.

Why VBC and not a bank?

Small businesses cannot get straight-up loans approved in today's economic climate as a start-up, or even as an established business. Companies who have no cash flow history, or inconsistent cash flows for the past several years, have to seek alternative financing. VBC specializes in loans through the U.S. Department of Agriculture Business and Industry Program (USDA), the Small Business Administration (SBA), and enormous commercial lenders that can take on risky non-bankable loans.

Why should I apply for a loan?

Businesses need accounts receivable financing and we can factor your receivables. Businesses also need equipment loans, refinancing existing debt, or real estate to build or expand a business.

Who are your customers?

Hotels, oil field service companies, long-term care centers, assisted living centers, franchises, manufacturing, sawmills, medical professionals and in general any operating company. We will look at any loan request. We cannot do them all, but we will surely try our best to get the loan request funded.

Is the application process complicated?

On any request to start, VBC simply needs these three pieces of information:

1. City and state where transaction is located
2. How much capital is requested
3. Specific use of the funds requested

We can factor your accounts receivable.

About Veillon Business Consulting, LLC

Veillon Business Consulting, LLC, (VBC) helps business start-ups, or expanding business owners to develop affordable strategies for growth, re-structure, and capitalization. VBC leverages R. Randy Veillon's 30+ years in banking and public finance.

VBC is a privately owned company founded in 2012. The owner and founder of the company, R. Randy Veillon, was supervisor of the Louisiana Economic Development Corporation loan guaranty program for 20 years. In addition, Mr. Veillon was a commercial banker for 11 years. He is also a graduate of the University of Louisiana in Lafayette, LA, a graduate of the School of Banking of the South at LSU, and a graduate with distinction of the Commercial Lending Graduate School at the University of Oklahoma.

VBC can help your business with:
- Business Planning
- Cash Flow Analysis
- Debt Restructure
- Connections to Banks and Alternative Lenders

Veillon Business Consulting, LLC, is extremely cost-effective and can save valuable time and aggravation preparing a business for capital raising and finding the right provider to close the deal. With one call, you can have access to VBC's extensive network of bankers and alternative lenders to find the one most likely to meet your needs. Simply put, *we simplify the lending process.*

Regardless whether you are a business in need of capital or a lending institution trying to find a way to say "yes" to more loan requests, our many years of experience with private and government loan programs can expedite the process of bringing both together to achieve their financial goals. If your business is a start-up and/or an expanding business that cannot get financing, then we can assist your bank with your loan request for the business. We can also find a bank to assist your business. We can do just about any loan of any size. If the business qualifies within our broad criteria, we will get the business loan approved.

We can perform accounts receivable, equipment, inventory and real estate financing. We can also factor your receivables.

We have numerous lenders all over the country who can do almost any loan request. Sometimes they participate with your local bank. These loans are available when your bank cannot do the loan due to its bank policy, or the bank does not have an interest in doing your loan request. In addition, we have close contacts with SBA, USDA and enormously large commercial loan lenders that can do any loan including real estate new construction, refinancing or long-term financing for owner occupied real estate, and financing for commercial real estate.

At Veillon Business Consulting, LLC we work with all legitimate funding programs available today, offering funding through hundreds of lenders. This gives you the best opportunity to get more funding at great terms. SBA Loans have never been easier for commercial real estate, debt refinance, or working capital with loans to $5 million, and repayment terms of 10 to 25 years. Take your business to the next level. Contact me and let's talk.

There are several ways a loan request can be completed. So, if you have a loan request that your bank has turned down, then stop right there and call us.

If you qualify, we will get your loan request approved. We will work diligently to put your loan request together for a quick approval.

If your loan gets stuck, reach for Veillon.
Better yet...start with us!
Office: 225.384.0760
Fax: 225.330.7328
E-mail: rveillon@veillonbusinessconsulting.com

About the Author

R. Randy Veillon, a native of Ville Platte, Louisiana, and a long time resident of Baton Rouge, served as the Program Manager of the Small Business Loan Program of the Louisiana Economic Development Corporation (LEDC), the agency that provides guaranties on commercial loans to banks. He has over 19 years' experience working for LEDC. He also assisted in the evaluation of new programs, while assisting with numerous LEDC incentive programs. Prior to LEDC, Randy worked in commercial banking for over 11 years. He is a graduate of the University of Louisiana in Lafayette, the LSU School of Banking of the South, and the Commercial Lending Graduate School at the University of Oklahoma with distinction. He is also a certified Economic Development Finance Professional.

Randy is a commercial loan broker, and owns Veillon Business Consulting, LLC, (VBC) that he started in 2012. Veillon Business Consulting believes that what is most important is not the money you make, but the money you *save*.

Veillon Business Consulting Services

1. **Connections to banks and alternative lenders –** No one can do it better or faster than VBC.

2. **Loans for start-up or expanding companies –** Like manufacturing, oil and gas companies, hotels, truck stops, real estate and more.

3. **Loan size from $200,000 to over $20 million**

4. **Extremely cost-effective –** Compare us to our competitors; no fees until you receive your loan proceeds.

5. **Financial expertise in the SBA, USDA and enormous size finance lenders –** And experience to set your business right for the future growth.

6. **Simple application process –** We need the city and state where the business is located, the capital required, and the purpose of the loan request to start the VBC process. We cannot help everyone, but will surely try our best on your specific business loan request.

If you qualify, Randy's team of experienced financial professionals can get your financial request approved. VBC will take care of your business as if it were our own.

Bankers: Send us your <u>turn-downs</u>. We may have a home for them.

Borrowers: Don't wait another minute. Apply today.

Contact Us
R. Randy Veillon, Sr.
Managing Partner

Veillon Business Consulting, LLC
P.O. Box 77512
Baton Rouge, LA 70879

Office: 225.384.0760
Fax: 225.330.7328
E-mail: rveillon@veillonbusinessconsulting.com